The Phantom Time Hypothesis

Hypothesis

A Chronological Conspiracy

Table of Contents

1. Introduction 1

2. Introduction to the Phantom Time Hypothesis 2

    2.1. The Genesis of Phantom Time 2

    2.2. Anomalies and Misalignments 3

    2.3. Contributions of Mathematics and Astronomy 3

    2.4. Architecture and Artifacts: Evidence or Contradictions? 4

    2.5. Implications for Historical Narratives 4

3. Heribert Illig: The Man Behind the Theory 6

    3.1. Unraveling the Tapestry of Time 6

    3.2. Illig's Groundbreaking Proposition 7

    3.3. The Thought Process and the Final Leap 7

    3.4. Illig and His Legacy 8

    3.5. Conclusion 8

4. Discrepancies in The Dark Ages: Anomalies Explored 9

    4.1. The Archival Abyss 9

    4.2. Architectural Anomalies 10

    4.3. Chronological Consternation 10

    4.4. Astronomical Apprehensions 11

    4.5. Numismatic Niggles 11

5. Assessing the Anomalous Artifacts 13

    5.1. The Inexplicable Gap in Architecture 13

    5.2. Warped Writings 13

    5.3. The Conundrum of Coinage 14

    5.4. Astronomical Anomalies 14

    5.5. Gregorian Calendar Mysteries 14

    5.6. Radiocarbon Dating Dilemma 15

6. Mysterious Mapmaking Exercises 16

7. Gregorian Reform: A Calendar Conspiracy? 17

7.1. The Julian Calendar: An Inaccurate Model of Time 17

7.2. The Gregorian Reform: A Chronological Leap 17

7.3. The Phantom Time Hypothesis: Unmasking a Potential

Fabrication 18

7.4. The Missing Years: An Elaborate Deception? 18

7.5. Wrapping up: Can We Trust our Calendars? 19

8. Astonishing Archaeology: Incongruities in Historical Record 21

8.1. The Missing Middles 21

8.2. Christian Architecture: Anomalous Chronology 22

8.3. Numismatic Enigmas 22

8.4. Radiocarbon Dating and Dendrochronology: Science in the

Service of History? 23

9. Chronological Critics: Perspectives against the Hypothesis 25

9.1. Countering Illegitimate Chronology 25

9.2. Insignificance of Archeological Strata 26

9.3. Tangible Artefacts and Documented Events 26

9.4. Interconnected Records and Global Histories 27

10. Supporting Stances: Who Believes in Phantom Time 29

10.1. The Conviction of Heribert Illig 29

10.2. Hans-Ulrich Niemitz and a Collaboration 30

10.3. The Cryptologist - Anatoly Fomenko 30

10.4. The Reception Among Conspiracists and Alternative

Historians 31

10.5. Broadening the Perspective 31

11. Implications of the Hypothesis: Rewriting History 32

11.1. The Effects on Chronology 32

11.2. Reevaluating Personalities and Events 33

11.3. Impact on Archaeology 33

11.4. Effect on Scientific Progress 34

11.5. Continuity of Power Structures 34

12. The Phantom Time Hypothesis: A Reflective Discourse 35

    12.1. Unveiling the Hypothesis 35

    12.2. The Foundation of The Hypothesis 36

    12.3. Historical Anomalies 36

    12.4. Opposition Against The Hypothesis 37

    12.5. The Intriguing Conclusion 37

Chapter 1. Introduction

Venture into one of the most intriguing theories of historical chronology in our Special Report on "The Phantom Time Hypothesis: A Chronological Conspiracy". This tantalizing concept suggests that several centuries of the Middle Ages may simply never have happened, and that we've been living a widespread historical falsehood. Far from a stuffy dissertation, this Special Report promises a fascinating journey, packed with cryptic clues, stunning installments of lost history, and gripping tales hinged on one man's audacious perspective of time. Our guiding prose invites all, from the ardent history buffs to the curious everyday readers, to explore this compelling proposition and ponder over the very fabric of history. Let's delve together into a conspiratorial narrative so extraordinary that it could reshape the way we perceive our past!

Chapter 2. Introduction to the Phantom Time Hypothesis

The Phantom Time Hypothesis is a proposal so daring, so jaw-dropping, it mandates a pause for contemplation. Prior to embarking on this intellectual voyage, it's imperative to fully comprehend the magnitude of the suggestion being made. According to this hypothesis, we currently live in the mid-eighteenth century, not the twenty-first century according to the Gregorian calendar. Circumventing nearly 300 years of falsehood calls for careful discourse and diligent analysis. To grasp this conjecture more concretely, let us plumb the depths of its origins, arguments, and implications.

2.1. The Genesis of Phantom Time

This conversation begins with Herbert Illig, a German publisher and historian. Prior to Illig, the existence—and absence—of the specified period had not been scrutinized to such mind-bending extremes. In 1991, Illig proposed an audacious theory: the period between 614 and 911 AD, often thought to be the Early Middle Ages, simply didn't exist. From Charlemagne to Harun al-Rashid, a span of nearly three centuries was a fabrication—an insertion that was never real.

Illig was influenced by the work of Hans-Ulrich Niemitz and other historians who had earlier begun questioning the established historical dating. Niemitz was particularly concerned with the Gregorian calendar reform of 1582 AD, and had started to ponder over why Pope Gregory XIII had removed ten days from the year, when the Julian calendar was only over by roughly 13 minutes each year.

2.2. Anomalies and Misalignments

The Phantom Time Hypothesis seeks to rationalize certain historical incongruities and anomalous events. By the dusk of the 8th century, Western Europe was presumably submerged in the Dark Ages—an epoch of socio-political decline following the collapse of the Western Roman Empire. As the 10th century dawned, however, the region seems to have miraculously leapt forwards in terms of society, culture and technology, commencing what is known as the Renaissance.

What explains this sudden surge of progress within a remarkably short span of time that was supposedly mired with socioeconomic deterioration? Illig noted a dearth of archaeological finds and reliable written records from this period, suggesting an artificially created historical buffer. The Phantom Time Hypothesis posits that this period of apparent darkness was, in fact, non-existent.

2.3. Contributions of Mathematics and Astronomy

It's prudent to delve deeper into the Gregorian calendar reform, which stokes the flames of this hypothesis's intrigue. By the 16th century, it had become apparent that the Julian calendar was in disarray, causing significant displacement of the dates of equinoxes and solstices. The adjustments made by Pope Gregory were to correct a 1,600-year accumulation of error amounting to about 13 days.

Illig and Niemitz, however, argue that the error eclipsed by the correction was actually closer to five days. Their contention is rooted in the difference between the Julian and tropical (solar) year lengths, the former being about 11 minutes longer each year. Over a millennium—1000 years—the discrepancy would account for roughly seven and a half days, not the ten days accounted for by Pope

Gregory.

2.4. Architecture and Artifacts: Evidence or Contradictions?

Close investigation of historical artifacts and architectural advancements from this alleged phantom era pose equally fascinating questions. Architecture, in particular, seems to take an abrupt and inexplicable leap forward after the 10th century. This remarkable transition from rudimentary Romanesque to sophisticated Gothic architecture leaves an undeniable question mark on the timeline of human progression.

Similarly, the relative scarcity of tangible artifacts and architectural evidences from these times amplifies the doubts raised by these historical and chronological conundrums. Illig and his adherents argue that this perceived vacuum is not evidence of cultural underdevelopment or decline, as generally accepted, but rather the straightforward fact that those centuries did not transpire.

2.5. Implications for Historical Narratives

Should the Phantom Time Hypothesis hold water, prominent historical narratives would unravel, and timelines would need to be refashioned. Personages like Charlemagne, who fall within the phantom timeline, might belong to the realm of myth and imagination, rather than history. Trade routes, political chronologies, genealogical trees, and cultural evolution would need reappraisal.

Expansive and peculiar as it may be, the Phantom Time Hypothesis invites us to scrutinize accepted frameworks of historical scholarship and question long-held beliefs. It propels us into an enthralling world where we must negotiate our understanding of time, history, and reality. While formidable, it also opens up endlessly engaging vistas of speculation and potential discovery.

As each layer of this hypothesis is peeled back, the reader must remain aware that it exists on the precipice between accepted history and radical reimagining. Let us continue to probe, explore, and question as we navigate the centuries bathed in phantom lights.

Chapter 3. Heribert Illig: The Man Behind the Theory

The birth of any idea often mirrors the spirit and persona of the individual who conceives it, just as it was with Heribert Illig, the man responsible for the Phantom Time Hypothesis. The audacious proposal of rewriting the calendar and deleting nearly three centuries from history is a grand reflection of Illig's unique perspective and intellectual prowess.

Born in 1947, in the Bavarian city of Vohenstrauß, Germany, Heribert Illig is not your typical time theorist. Trained as a Germanist and economist, Illig cut his teeth in the world of academia and swiftly distinguished himself as a formidable and lustrous mind. However, his passion lay elsewhere, towards the intriguing domain of historical anomaly and chronology.

3.1. Unraveling the Tapestry of Time

His fascination with historical chronology first manifested in 1986 when he, along with two other chronology critics, Hans-Ulrich Niemitz and Manfred Zeller, co-founded the German Society for Ancient Studies (Deutsche Gesellschaft für Vor- und Frühgeschichte). Their alliance laid the foundation for a daring pursuit of reevaluating accepted historical timelines.

Adventurous, unconventive, and unabashedly critical, Illig's interactions with historical records were always one step removed from the accepted wisdom. He soon learned that one must dig beneath the surface of scholarly explanations to unearth the truth lurking underneath. His training in economics and Germanic studies lent Illig a certain analytical rigor, combined with an unconventional perspective - a perfect recipe to challenge prevailing historical narratives.

3.2. Illig's Groundbreaking Proposition

In the 1990s, Illig began to develop the Phantom Time Hypothesis. This audacious premise suggests the Early Middle Ages (614–911 A.D.) never transpired, and nearly 300 years of our accepted history were an elaborate fabrication.

This proposition drew heavily on the work of Jean Hardouin, a 17th-century Benedictine monk who claimed that all texts, documents, and artefacts dating from ancient Rome to his time were forged by a group of monastic scholars. Illig expanded on Hardouin's ideas, drawing upon the perceived inadequacies of the Gregorian calendar and striking evidence from the disciplines of archaeology, architecture, and history – all packaging them in a compelling theory that challenges centuries of belief.

3.3. The Thought Process and the Final Leap

Illig was irked by inconsistencies and gaps in historical records of the Early Middle Ages, particularly in Roman and Byzantine history. His intellectual curiosity was further pricked by the supposed discrepancy in the Julian and Gregorian calendars. Pope Gregory XIII's introduction of the new calendar in 1582 allowed for a 10-day correction to reinstate the spring equinox to March 21. This recalculation, according to Illig, should have amounted to a 13-day correction if the Julian calendar had been in continuous use since its inception in 45 B.C. The unaccounted three days pointed towards the existence of 'phantom time.'

His ideas, however revolutionary, were not accepted without criticism, generating a mixture of reactions ranging from intrigue to outright rejection. Nevertheless, Illig remained steadfast in his conviction, continuing to elaborate on his postulates with an unwavering belief in their veracity.

3.4. Illig and His Legacy

To this day, the Phantom Time Hypothesis continues to confound scholars, generate debates, and fascinate history enthusiasts. As the creator of such an audacious theory, Illig's legacy goes beyond creating ripples in conventional historical analysis – he poses a challenge. A challenge not only to our understanding of time but our willingness to question, investigate, and seek the truth beyond the given. His reimagining of history encourages us all to look beyond the surface, to question, and challenge accepted wisdom, ultimately pushing the boundaries of scholarship and intellectual inquiry.

3.5. Conclusion

Heribert Illig's journey, from a studious Germanist and economist to the creator of one of the most intriguing theories of historical chronology, is not just a chronicle of intellectual courage. It serves as a reminder that audacious ideas and scholarly skepticism can comfortably coexist. Despite the widespread rejection of his theory, Illig stands tall as a figure of robust critique, intellectual exploration, and indelible curiosity, sculpting a legacy that continues to inspire debate and inspire those willing to venture beyond conventional wisdom.

Chapter 4. Discrepancies in The Dark Ages: Anomalies Explored

The genesis of the Phantom Time Hypothesis is rooted in the discrepancies found throughout the Dark Ages, a nebulous period that, by definition, seems to persist in obscurity, providing endless fuel for investigation and skepticism alike. Adherents of this theory see shadows where others see illumination, tracing peculiar inconsistencies and anomalies that cloak this epoch with an indelible sense of mystery. Let's delve into the arcane depths of these perceived aberrations and understand what makes the believers claim that the Dark Ages, or at least a significant chunk of it, never actually occurred.

4.1. The Archival Abyss

Historical records serve as lifelines to our past, guiding us through the mazes of history, weaving a timeline that forms the backbone of our understanding of bygone eras. However, for the span approximated between 7th and 10th centuries AD, there exists a seemingly cavernous gap; a period less represented in written annals as compared to centuries immediately preceding and succeeding it.

Dearth of substantial contemporaneous written chronicles from this era, often attributed to societal decay or transitions, has raised intrigue among proponents of the Phantom Time Hypothesis. These theorists maintain that the striking archival scarcity indicates, not a period of declining literary pursuits, but a nonexistent timeframe invented by chronologists and historians.

4.2. Architectural Anomalies

Another significant strand of thought enveloping the Phantom Time Hypothesis pertains to anachronistic architectural advances attributed to the Dark Ages. A structural leap, distinctly observable in art, architecture, and technological innovations, transpired around the 10th century AD, a progression too abrupt - the theory argues - to be the result of organic evolution.

This alleged break in the architectural continuum posits that the techniques and styles seen in constructions attributed to the Dark Ages were too advanced to be a refinement of earlier styles, but seemed more derivative of later periods, feeding Phantom Time Hypothesis's assertions that these 'dark' centuries were artificially interpolated.

4.3. Chronological Consternation

The Julian calendar, devised in 45 BC, was acknowledged to have a computational flaw: a surplus of approximately 10.8 minutes per year, leading to a surplus day roughly every 128 years. By the time of Pope Gregory XIII (16th century), under whose pontificate the Gregorian calendar was established, this equated to around 13 surplus days - if we consider an uninterrupted progression from Julius Caesar through the 'missing' Dark Ages.

However, when the papal bull Inter Gravissimas brought forth the Gregorian calendar in 1582, only ten days were removed. To Phantom Time theorists, this points to a discrepancy - there appears to be a shortfall of about 297 years. This gap aligns almost perfectly with the proposed phantom timeperiod, adding another element of mystery to the chronological conjecture.

4.4. Astronomical Apprehensions

Evidence in the realm of celestial observations also feeds the Phantom Time Hypothesis. Historical accounts of solar and lunar eclipses, comets, and other astronomical phenomena purportedly from this era are rare, and many documented events prove irreproducible using astronomical retrocalculation. For instance, the detailed accounts of the eclipses recorded by Pliny in his 'Naturalis Historia' fail to correspond to any calculable date.

Phantom Time proponents argue that these inaccurate accounts suggest a fabrication of events to validate the existence of a period that was never observed, thus adding yet another compelling dimension to their proposition.

4.5. Numismatic Niggles

Finally, we delve into the numismatic evidence - an essential tool for historians in the validation of historical periods. The scarcity of coins from this era, particularly Charlemagne's rule, ignite the flame of suspicion at the heart of the Phantom Time Hypothesis. Counterarguments cite the possible loss or damage of these objects over time. However, proponents of the theory insist that the rareness and uncharacteristic style of coins found suggest a later fabrication.

In summary, the Dark Ages hold an enticing shroud of mystery and intrigue that perpetuates the Phantom Time Hypothesis. By tracing discrepancies in the written archives, architectural progression, chronological computation, celestial observations, and numismatic data, adherents of the theory contend that these so-called 'Dark Ages' were, in fact, a brightly illuminated fiction, casting shadowy doubt on our understanding of history. As we unravel these intriguing suggestions, we venture further into the labyrinth of this mind-bending theory. The jury is still out, and perhaps, in such exploratory ventures, the journey is indeed more illuminating than the destination.

Chapter 5. Assessing the Anomalous Artifacts

Examining a thread of enigmatic artifacts etched into the timeline will help us discern this intricately woven tapestry of narratives and counter-narratives. The aim is to lift the veils shrouding the historical anomalies that the Phantom Time Hypothesis so daringly thrusts into our collective consciousness.

5.1. The Inexplicable Gap in Architecture

The Middle Ages, stretching from the 7th to the 10th centuries, exists as an epoch of remarkable architectural evolution. Or, at least, it's supposed to. When uncovering the characteristics defining each architectural era, a puzzling continuity from the Romanesque right up to the Gothic period surfaces. Rather disconcertingly, scarce are the artifacts embodying the architectural flavor characteristic of the supposed Early Middle Ages. This unexplained break feeds the Phantom Time Hypothesis' postulation, catapulting us into a realm where conventional wisdom is rendered questionable at best.

5.2. Warped Writings

The continuity of literature and written records is another field seemingly plagued by inconsistency. Drastic stylistic changes over different eras feature as expected, however, the so-called Dark Ages display disturbingly little evolution. Was writing simply stalling during this epoch? Or, more intriguingly, did these centuries fail to witness the birth of any substantial literature because, as the Phantom Time Hypothesis proffers, they simply never occurred?

5.3. The Conundrum of Coinage

The meticulous process of coinage, closely tied to the ruling power, reveals telling insight into the chronological ebb and flow. Yet, if we meticulously navigate through numismatic records, a perplexing panorama emerges. There appears to be a consistent, inexplicable gap in the lineage of coins, especially between the Antiquity and the Middle Ages. This peculiar silence resonates with the ostensible chronological conspiracy as a tempting validation of the Phantom Time Hypothesis.

5.4. Astronomical Anomalies

Moving beyond terrestrial traces, astronomical records too seem to corroborate this audacious hypothesis. Historical descriptions and depictions of celestial events, when compared against modern scientific computation, show unsettling discrepancies. Comet sightings, lunar and solar eclipses jotted down during the paradoxical period don't line up with their predicted timelines. The Phantom Time Hypothesis posits that such anomalies are far from random errors, but rather, they are the whispers of a forgotten or misinterpreted reality.

5.5. Gregorian Calendar Mysteries

The Gregorian calendar, upon which our daily lives are consistently regulated, presents another intriguing puzzle piece. Instituted by Pope Gregory XIII in 1582 to rectify the inaccuracies of the Julian calendar, discrepancies suggest it may have overcompensated the correction by a good 300 years. The convenient hypothesis: those 300 years were added to anchor the fabricated timeline espoused by historians, thus buttressing this daring theory.

5.6. Radiocarbon Dating Dilemma

The cornerstone of modern archaeology, radiocarbon dating is regarded as an unequivocal witness to the age of history's relics. But what if the reliability of this seemingly infallible discipline came under question? A nagging inconsistency in radiocarbon dating of organic materials from the alleged Phantom Time period ignites reconsideration of its omnipotent status in archaeology, offering some credence to the theory under investigation.

Chapter 6. Mysterious Mapmaking Exercises

In the labyrinth of geography and cartography, anomalous maps of the supposed Phantom period are another intriguing paradox to unravel. Detailed cartographic records overlap and blur, reiterating the continuity quirk instead of laying out a clear chronology. Could this be compelling evidence of a manipulated timeline?

Deem the exploration of these anomalous artifacts not as an endorsement of the Phantom Time Hypothesis, but as an invitation to question. To think in uncharted territories and expand the horizons of understanding beyond convention. This dive into historical artifacts is less about proving or debunking this radical theory and more about exploring the infallibility of data and questioning preconceived notions. These enigmatic relics, whispered tales, and cryptic calendars constitute a chapter in the ongoing investigation — a quest to sift truth from assumed reality. Whether they serve to expose phantom years or lay bare our limitations in interpretation, each artifact holds a key to unlocking deeper understanding. The past, it seems, is always ready to unveil novel stories, given we're prepared to listen with an open mind.

Chapter 7. Gregorian Reform: A Calendar Conspiracy?

Before venturing into the thick of our discussion, we must set the stage. The year is 1582. Pope Gregory XIII, buoyed by his ecclesiastical authority, announces a significant reform to the Julian calendar, which has been in place for over a millennium. This alteration, encompassing a shift from the Julian to the Gregorian calendar (named after the Pope himself), constitutes a key element of the Phantom Time Hypothesis.

7.1. The Julian Calendar: An Inaccurate Model of Time

Primarily speaking, the Julian calendar, initiated by Julian the Great in 45 BC, inflicted a small yet significant error — it overestimated the solar year by 11 minutes and 14 seconds. This apparent trifle, when accumulated over centuries, led to a substantial discrepancy between the calendar's date and the actual solar year.

Under the Julian calendar, the spring equinox floated back into earlier and earlier calendar days, misaligning the dates of Christian holidays, most notably Easter. This was unacceptable to the Papacy, prompting Pope Gregory XIII to remedy this inconvenience by introducing a correction to the calendar.

7.2. The Gregorian Reform: A Chronological Leap

According to official history, the Gregorian reform proposed a leap of ten days. October 4, 1582, was followed by October 15, 1582. This, it was argued, would realign the calendar with the solar year, bringing the equinox back to its 'proper' place and allowing Easter to be celebrated at the 'correct' time.

But herein lies the crux of our discussion — could this move have potentially been a cover-up for a substantial chronological conspiracy? The Phantom Time Hypothesis posits that the calendar reform aimed not to rectify a small drifting of days, but rather to bridge a chasm between actual history and a fictional concoction of several centuries.

7.3. The Phantom Time Hypothesis: Unmasking a Potential Fabrication

According to German historian Heribert Illig, who put forth the Phantom Time Hypothesis in 1991, the Gregorian reform was an attempt to cover up a fabrication of history that spanned three centuries. He contends that the years 614 AD to 911 AD never really existed in history, and were simply introduced into the chronological records to account for events and figures that were either fictional or misdated.

Illig argues that this leap of ten days was rather exaggerated. Instead, he opines, there should have been a discrepancy of thirteen days if all the calendar drifting from the Julian system was accounted for. With this speculation, he raises the idea of a calendar conspiracy, questioning the authenticity of a sizable chunk of medieval history.

7.4. The Missing Years: An Elaborate Deception?

The evidence backing up this radical hypothesis may initially seem tenuous but is thought-provoking indeed. Illig points out inconsistencies in historical documentation, architectural anachronisms, and the dearth of archeological evidence corresponding to a given time period. One of the most controversial examples mentioned by Illig relates to the reign of Charlemagne, a significant figure of the purportedly fictional era, whom Illig considers to be a myth or possibly a blend of several persons from different epochs.

Many historians dismiss the Phantom Time Hypothesis as eccentric or outright absurd, unable to reconcile Illig's audacious hypothesis with the wealth of historical knowledge and layered complexities of international dating systems, historical documents, and astronomical observations.

7.5. Wrapping up: Can We Trust our Calendars?

While mainstream academia rejects the Phantom Time Hypothesis, the questions it poses about our perception of historical time are certainly challenging. Is it truly possible that our calendar was intentionally manipulated to accommodate false centuries, thus presenting to the world an elaborate historical simulation? Or are these nothing more than brazen allegations that uncomfortably challenge our established historical timeline?

Pope Gregory XIII's reform may forever be a significant historical event in our collective memory. But through the lens of the Phantom Time Hypothesis, this calendar correction takes on a new dimension, stirring us to question the very passage of historical time, the evidence that seeks to represent that passage, and most strikingly, our steadfast belief in historical chronology.

In conclusion, whether the Gregorian reform was part of a larger conspiracy or a mere rectification of a solar year discrepancy remains open for interpretation. Despite the skepticism it faces, the Phantom Time Hypothesis continues to offer an audacious exploration of historical chronology, peeling back layers of accepted history to reveal a potential realm of shadows lurking beneath the surface of our accepted timeline.

Chapter 8. Astonishing Archaeology: Incongruities in Historical Record

The debate on the validity and authenticity of centuries passed is not simply confined to the halls of academia or the pages of scholarly journals. The evidence, or lack thereof, can often be found in physical spaces that we have decades, even centuries, of human activity imprinted upon. In our journey through the phantom time hypothesis, the inconsistencies in archaeology offer some of the most provocative speculation.

8.1. The Missing Middles

Perhaps the most glaring concern arising from the phantom time hypothesis is the seemingly missing bits of monumental and everyday structures that should represent the era allegedly fabricated, particularly from the 7th to 10th centuries. When one examines historical buildings and settlements in Europe, the most intriguing facet is the noticeable absence of architecturally distinctive Carolingian and Ottonian buildings, typically associated with the alleged phantom time period.

Western Europe saw stylistic tectonic shifts from the preceding Romanesque and ensuing Gothic architectural styles. Yet, despite the profound sociopolitical changes reported during the supposedly false Middle Ages, such as Charlemagne's reign or the initiation of the Holy Roman Empire, there seems to be a distinct lack of physical structures reflecting these epochs. Society appears to have jumped from antiquity structures directly into the High Medieval period.

Several high-profile instances compound this issue. For example, Charlemagne's Palace of Aachen, one of the most celebrated architectural feats of the time, exhibits styles and techniques significantly in advance for a structure supposedly constructed in the 8th century. Some even question the originality of the palatine chapel and whether it was built by Charlemagne at all.

8.2. Christian Architecture: Anomalous Chronology

A closer assessment of early Christian architecture further fuels the mystery. It displays an inexplicable inconsistency with the widely accepted historical timeline - the sudden emergence of the Pre-Romanesque style in the 10th century without a clear progression from the architecture of Late Antiquity.

Most Romanesque churches appear to have been constructed before or just after 1000 A.D. Prior to this, we find a dearth of Christian structures attributable to the phantom time period. The churches we do have from an earlier date, notably the Merovingian churches, substantially differ in style and building technique, bearing closer resemblance to ancient Roman temples.

Moreover, closer examination of these supposedly early Christian churches often reveals that certain parts believed to be original are, in fact, later additions or restorations. The discrepancies in style, material, and technique, hidden under layers of renovations, do little to help squelch the phantom time controversy.

8.3. Numismatic Enigmas

The study of historical coins further emphasizes the incongruity. European coinage underwent a substantial transformation in the Middle Ages. Still, a peculiar disruption in the gradual evolution of coin styles can be observed, consistent with the phantom time hypothesis.

In contrast to the widespread use of gold in Roman times, coins from the speculated phantom time are predominantly silver or bronze. The gold penny introduced by Charlemagne around 794 and the subsequent widespread use of silver in European coinage, established in the late 10th century, present sudden, unexplained shifts in monetary practices. They disrupt the linear progression in economic history and pose tough questions for critics of the phantom time hypothesis.

8.4. Radiocarbon Dating and Dendrochronology: Science in the Service of History?

Scientific dating techniques have long served as allied weapons in the fight against the phantom time hypothesis. Radiocarbon dating and dendrochronology—tree-ring dating—have particularly been used in an attempt to authenticate the traditional chronological timeline. However, these techniques have faced their share of criticism and proven far from infallible.

Radiocarbon dating, which measures the decay of Carbon-14 in organic materials, often yields dates that fortify the traditional timeline. But critics of this technique cite its susceptibility to environmental factors, while pointing out that different dating labs can produce wildly divergent dates for the same artifact.

Equally contentious is dendrochronology. By correlating wide and narrow tree-ring growth patterns across existing samples, this method can theoretically date wooden objects or structures. Still, skepticism arises from the practice of 'wiggle-matching' and the inherent subjectivity in reconciling discrepancies between samples.

Finally, it's important to note that while these methods may provide a date range, they cannot, with absolute certainty, confirm the set historical timeframe we follow. They merely uphold a possibility within a broader context of uncertainty.

In sum, both the realms of archaeology and numismatic study, coupled with considerations from architecture and scientific dating techniques, pose intriguing questions and fuel the debate surrounding the phantom time hypothesis. As we continue to probe the depths of historical record, these inconsistencies serve not as definitive proof, but as tantalizing suggestions that something could indeed be amiss in the accepted chronology of our past. The phantom time hypothesis, while contentious, remains a conspiracy not easily dismissed.

Chapter 9. Chronological Critics: Perspectives against the Hypothesis

Despite the allure of the Phantom Time Hypothesis with its labyrinth of beguiling suppositions, there exists a multitude of scholars and academics who take a dissenting perspective. In order to ensure a comprehensive and balanced discussion, we must put these diverging views under the microscope, spanning rigorous scholarly debates to common objections raised against the hypothesis.

9.1. Countering Illegitimate Chronology

Foremost among many critics' arguments is the assertion that Illig, the main proponent of the Phantom Time Hypothesis, fundamentally misinterprets the chronology of the Middle Ages. Illig posits that Holy Roman Emperor Otto III, with collaboration from Pope Sylvester II, deliberately extended the calendar to place themselves in the year 1000 AD. Critics, however, note that plenty of verifiable artifacts and accounts date back to the alleged "phantom time," thereby contradicting the hypothesis.

First, there are numerous independently verifiable astronomical events recorded during this period. Many safely dated historical documents allude to occurrences like solar eclipses or the passing of Halley's comet — events that can be precisely calculated backward using celestial mechanics. These accounts provide robust testimony to the progression of time as we understand it today.

Second, the absence of corresponding time gaps in other historical timelines is a significant obstacle to the hypothesis. For instance, the

Chinese, Byzantine, and Arabic histories do not share a simultaneous 'blank period.' Would not a 297-year historical fabrication require immensely significant global conspiracy?

9.2. Insignificance of Archeological Strata

Arguably, Illeg and his followers point to discrepancies in the archaeological record as evidence to support their hypothesis, particularly in the apparent scarcity of architectural achievements during the 7th to 10th-century period. Critics, however, highlight several damning counter-arguments.

For one, stratigraphy — the forerunner method of conventional sequencing — cannot alone provide precise dating. It is less a mathematical or mechanical instrument and more of an interpretative tool, dependent on the contextual information available. Further details are often gleaned through other dating methods such as dendrochronology or radiocarbon dating, neither of which support the Phantom Time Hypothesis.

Furthermore, a seeming void of architecture or art does not conclusively indicate a gap in time. It could reflect a quiet era of economic or demographic downturn, religious changes impacting construction styles, or increased use of perishable materials, among other equally plausible explanations.

9.3. Tangible Artefacts and Documented Events

Illeg's theory crumbles when considering the overflow of documented events, from battles to royal weddings, and physical relics like coins, statues, and parchment scrolls, all inevitably dated to the alleged phantom years. Remember, these are entities constructed, engraved, and written in stone, metal, and vellum - their existence unalterable and non-negotiable.

Many such historical assets exist worldwide, curated in libraries, museums, and national archives. By scrutinizing such items, historians and archaeologists can employ a wide array of dating techniques, and overwhelmingly, these methods invalidate the Phantom Time Hypothesis.

Even the tree-ring patterns across Europe form an unbroken chain, stretching back more than 10,000 years. The remarkable consistency of dendrochronological data across different geographical locations makes it highly unlikely that nearly three centuries could just simply disappear undetected.

9.4. Interconnected Records and Global Histories

Lastly, one cannot ignore the multitudes of contemporaneous histories outside Europe. It strains credulity to argue that so many disparate civilizations, each with its own sophisticated system of keeping history, could somehow coordinate to erase or manipulate centuries of shared human experience.

According to Illig's proposition, countries like China, India, and civilizations in the Middle East would have to have fabricated the same three centuries, including dynastic shifts, trade transactions, and astronomical observations. The logistical impossibility of such an extensive global conspiracy adds significant weight to the critics' case.

In conclusion, while the Phantom Time Hypothesis is a thrilling philosophical and historical adventure, a broad range of diverse and robust evidence exists that contradicts this outlandish proposition. Critics, armed with compelling arguments and tangible proof, make a persuasive case for dismissing the hypothesis. Time, it would seem, flows undeterred by human interference, leaving the tales of phantom years as an intriguing anomaly in the annals of historical conjecture.

Chapter 10. Supporting Stances: Who Believes in Phantom Time

The veracity of the Phantom Time Hypothesis, coined by German historian Heribert Illig, is shrouded in ambiguity, cradled by a handful, and robustly contested by most of the mainstream academia. Despite this, Illig isn't isolated in this phenomenon. A minor but resilient group of scholars and enthusiasts from various fields have approached the theory with curiosity, receptivity, and even gravitation.

10.1. The Conviction of Heribert Illig

The origins of the Phantom Time Hypothesis are tangled with the life and works of Heribert Illig. His initial devotion to conventional historical interpretations gradually yielded to doubts. Unaccounted inconsistencies and gaps between archaeological findings and written histories began to gnaw at his trust in the established narrative. This unique exploration fortuitously dovetailed with the works of two other scholars, Christoph Marx and Hans-Ulrich Niemitz. Together, they laid the foundation of the Phantom Time Hypothesis, suggesting that the years 614-911 AD perhaps never existed.

Illig's conviction was bolstered by evidence that seemed to excavate the lack of tangible history during this period. Key among his concerns were the scarcely verifiable construction dates of Charlemagne's Aachen Palace, the reportedly 'forged' documents of the Holy Roman Empire, an alleged cover-up by Pope Sylvester II, and the enactment of the Gregorian calendar. This calculated chronology manipulation, Illig believed, was to vindicate an 'artificially established millennium'.

10.2. Hans-Ulrich Niemitz and a Collaboration

The alignment of the phantom time concept with Hans-Ulrich Niemitz's work was fortuitous. Prior to his encounter with Illig, Niemitz had delved into the discrepancies surrounding early medieval architecture dating. His findings dovetailed with Illig's hypothesis in a way that one might liken to two pieces of a puzzle coming together.

Niemitz made a significant contribution to the theory, arguing that the timeline combination of Byzantine and Islamic history with the Julian and Gregorian calendars substantiated the claim of the 'phantom' centuries. His studies of radiocarbon dating also unveiled anomalies that reinforced doubts about the established historical timelines during 600-900 AD.

10.3. The Cryptologist - Anatoly Fomenko

Perhaps the most surprising support comes from Anatoly Fomenko, a Russian mathematician and cryptologist. Fomenko's influence in the Phantom Time Hypothesis, although not direct, serves to validate some of its underpinnings. Fomenko's New Chronology postulates that conventional chronology is brutally flawed, arguing that most known historical events occurred significantly later in history, compressing the timeline. Some proponents of Illig's theory view Fomenko's approach as a form of endorsement, despite Fomenko's argument that history began around 800 AD, which contradicts the phantom time frame.

10.4. The Reception Among Conspiracists and Alternative Historians

The Phantom Time Hypothesis has, predictably, generated appreciable traction within the community of conspiracists and alternative historians. Note the works of authors such as Philip Coppens, who regularly cast doubt on mainstream historical narratives. This theory nurtures an essential part of their convictions – the idea that history has been deliberately distorted to serve particular agendas.

The seemingly outlandish nature of the Phantom Time Hypothesis theory might make it palatable only to contrarians, but the support it has received echoes an enduring human curiosity for the quest of understanding time, history, and our place in it. The divergence of these perspectives challenges us not to blindly accept, but to vigorously scrutinize our views.

10.5. Broadening the Perspective

The Phantom Time Hypothesis might oscillate between enigmatic and incredulous in its current form, but should it garner more empirical proof, this theory might gain wider acceptance. The following sections would dive into the denials and dismissals of the hypothesis.

While this speculative branch of historical chronology remains on the fringe, its implications probe our fundamental understanding of historical integrity. It provokes a critical reconsideration of time, pushing us to question our ancestral narratives and the intellectual and ceremonial structures that have scaffolded them for centuries.

Chapter 11. Implications of the Hypothesis: Rewriting History

The Phantom Time Hypothesis, postulated by German historian Heribert Illig, is a drastic reappraisal of accepted historical timelines. According to Illig, the years AD 614 to 911 were entirely fabricated in an elaborate deception coordinated by the Holy Roman Emperor Otto III and Pope Sylvester II. This hypothesis posits that we're not in the 21st century but rather sometime in the 18th. This assertion has immense repercussions on how we understand and interpret history, requiring an extensive rethink of well-established historical narratives and archaeological records.

11.1. The Effects on Chronology

If we accept the Phantom Time Hypothesis as true, historical chronology as we know it would need to be dramatically reconfigured. That means, nearly three centuries of dynastic successions, wars, political changes, cultural developments, scientific progress, and socioeconomic transformations considered as milestones in our human story would be wiped away - negating their influence on the subsequent years.

Furthermore, three centuries' worth of religious movements, architectural achievements, and legal advancements would have to be re-examined or invalidated. For instance, the events surrounding Islam's founding and expansion, the age of the Vikings, and the inception of feudalism in Europe would need to be entirely reconsidered, substantially rewriting our understanding of religious, military, and socio-political evolution.

11.2. Reevaluating Personalities and Events

A substantial alteration in the timeline tightens the temporal proximity of documented historical figures who, under the established timeline, are believed to have lived centuries apart. This insight would precipitate an upending of our understanding of cultural and intellectual influences, potentially leading to new and fascinating connections between key historical figures, their ideas, and the world they affected.

Similarly, events believed to have occurred in the 'phantom' centuries would either be thrust into another time period or considered complete fabrications. Consider Charlemagne, the founder of the Carolingian Empire, who ruled during one of the supposedly 'phantom' centuries. Has his life been a historic mirage, or should we place his reign and the significant changes he brought to Europe in a different era?

11.3. Impact on Archaeology

The consequences on archaeological dating methods are vast. Tangible artefacts and structures dated to the disputed years would need to be subjected to alternative dating methods. This might shift their historical significance or imply that they belong to other epochs, effectively sending shockwaves through the world of archaeology.

For example, Aachen Cathedral, built during Charlemagne's reign, revered as an archaeological treasure, would be thrown into chronological disarray. The signature synthesis of Roman, Carolingian and Ottonian, architecture may need to be ascribed to a different period, or the cathedral could be earmarked as a prodigious chronological fraud.

11.4. Effect on Scientific Progress

Scientific advances nurtured over the Phantom Time Hypothesis period must then belong to other epochs too. With the supposed absence of those three centuries, scientific progress from other time periods may have transpired more rapidly than we initially believed. Innovations attributed to the supposedly non-existent period, like the codification of the modern calendar system by Pope Gregory XIII or the astronomical developments by Anglo-Saxon monk Bede, would need to be reconsidered.

11.5. Continuity of Power Structures

Finally, the deceptive nature inherent in the Phantom Time Hypothesis raises inevitable questions about the power structures that may have contrived this vast chronologic fraud. A speculated motive for this manipulation claims Otto III wanted to artificially construct the year AD 1000 in his reign. But such an assertion implies a colluded mastery of manipulation between Church and Empire, which impacts our understanding of the dynamics of power, faith, and image-building during the Middle Ages, and perhaps beyond.

In conclusion, the Phantom Time Hypothesis strikes at the heart of our chronologic understanding—posing dramatic implications for historiography, archaeology, and the very fabric of societal evolution. Few theories have the potential to so completely rewrite history. Even if the hypothesis ultimately fails to gain mainstream acceptance, the questioning and scrutiny it invites are valuable processes in our search for historical truth.

Chapter 12. The Phantom Time Hypothesis: A Reflective Discourse

The Phantom Time Hypothesis carves its niche in historical chronology with a hypothesis that revives a shadow question in the minds of many history enthusiasts: Did the Early Middle Ages really happen? Introduced by Heribert Illig in 1991, this theory begs a provocative reevaluation of the endorsed chronology we've long adhered to.

12.1. Unveiling the Hypothesis

The Phantom Time Hypothesis claims that the years 614 to 911 AD, geographically known as the Early Middle Ages, were fabricated and did not engender the historical events we've been led to believe. Proponents of the hypothesis argue that these 297 years—the phantom time—are practically little more than a figmentation of the imagination, given birth due to the synchronization of the historical record by corrupt or inept scholars of the past.

Ecclesiastically, this period is marked by the rise of Islam in the Middle East, gradual Christianization of the Germanic tribes in Northern Europe, the reign of Charlemagne and the Carolingian Renaissance that supposedly followed. However, Phantom Time advocates pose disturbing uncertainties around these event sequences, suggesting a chronological invention rather than a faithful recording of history.

12.2. The Foundation of The Hypothesis

The cornerstone of the Phantom Time Hypothesis was the Gregorian calendar reform of 1582. The inadequacy of Julian calendar to maintain synchrony with the Tropical year lead to a drift of about 10 days by the time of Pope Gregory XIII. To rectify the anomaly, he induced the celebrated calendar reform, causing October 4, 1582, to be followed by October 15, 1582, effectively excising ten days from the historical record.

Skeptics, including Illig, swiftly pointed out a discrepancy: the Julian calendar, instituted by Julius Caesar in 46 BC, accounted for an annual excess of roughly 11 minutes — an error amounting to 13 days over the course of 1,627 years. Therefore, by 1582, the calendar should have been out of step by 13 days, and not ten as the Gregorian reform considered.

12.3. Historical Anomalies

Supporting this peculiar stance are a few documented historical anomalies that feed the ambiguity. Firstly, the paucity of architectural activity and significant historical manuscripts derived from the purported phantom time. This dearth of cultural remnants raises legitimate questions on the existence of the era.

Secondly, the unpredictable proliferation of art, literature, philosophy, and technology, known as the Carolingian Renaissance under Charlemagne, seems unlikely to have found its ground in a supposedly barbarian Europe of the 8th century AD. It feels abrupt and anachronistic to the gradual refinement typically associated with societal growth.

Furthermore, the evolution of the Julian calendar into the Gregorian, featuring a mere three-day correction instead of a requisite thirteen, fuels suspicions around a probable insertion of 297 non-existent years.

12.4. Opposition Against The Hypothesis

No conjecture so bold goes without acquiring powerful counterarguments. Mainstream historians and archeologists contest the Phantom Time Hypothesis both vociferously and convincingly, utilizing both documentary and physical evidence to uphold the familiar narrative.

Linkages with independently verified Chinese, Middle Eastern, and American Mesoamerican chronologies reveal a timeline consistent with conventional European history. Moreover, recorded sightings of solar eclipses and Halley's Comet, well-corroborated across civilizations, contradict the theorized chronological manipulation. Significant inventions, such as the stirrup, and architectural advances during the alleged phantom time further challenge the hypothesis.

12.5. The Intriguing Conclusion

In unveiling the Phantom Time Hypothesis, complexities beyond a linear understanding of historical chronology emerge, swathing the Early Middle Ages in an aura of thrilling mystery. While the bulk of evidence lies in favor of the status quo, this audacious theory stirs our curiosity and impels us to scrutinize the architectural artifacts, recorded history, calendar calculations, and other tethering factors of the era more critically.

Whether you cleave to Illig's perspective or remain loyal to the traditional understanding, the probe into the Phantom Time Hypothesis is an enlightening venture into the labyrinth of human chronology and an engaging encounter with the concept of historical time itself. Despite its untenable footing in academic spheres, the hypothesis ultimately adds a vertiginous new depth to the study and appreciation of historical chronology.

Printed in Great Britain
by Amazon